FreshAire

BY CHIP DAVIS
COMPOSED BY CHIP DAVIS

Piano reductions and editing by Jackson Berkey

ISBN 978-0-7935-3742-6

Published by Dots And Lines Ink
9130 Mormon Bridge Road, Omaha, NE 68152 (402) 457-4341

DISTRIBUTED BY

 HAL•LEONARD™

7777 W. BLUEMOUND RD. P.O. BOX 13819 MILWAUKEE, WI 53213

Prelude

PIANO REDUCTION AND EDITING
BY JACKSON BERKEY

COMPOSED BY CHIP DAVIS

SEGUE TO **Chocolate Fudge**

* Ed. note: Start with a full pedal and release slowly, as indicated by dotted line.

Chocolate Fudge

PIANO REDUCTION AND EDITING
BY JACKSON BERKEY

COMPOSED BY CHIP DAVIS

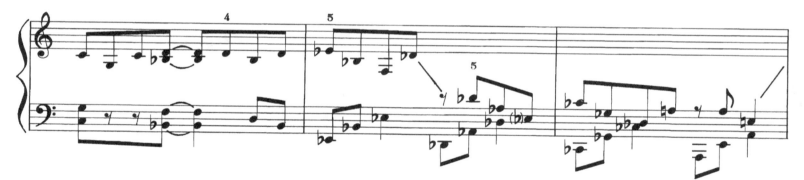

3

less staccato

staccato, as before

4

8va bassa 2nd time - - - - - - - - - - - - - - - -

Interlude 1

PIANO REDUCTION AND EDITING
BY JACKSON BERKEY

COMPOSED BY CHIP DAVIS

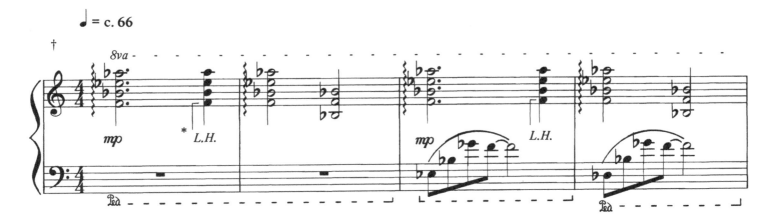

† Interlude 1 uses a 4-note ostinato pattern in the right hand.

* Take bottom note of chord in left hand, as indicated.

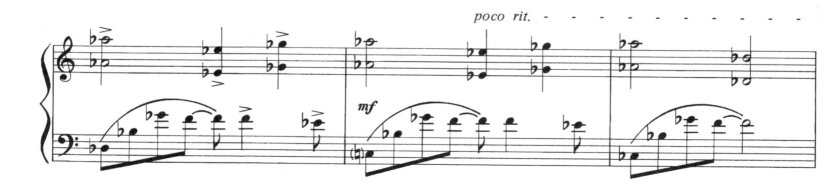

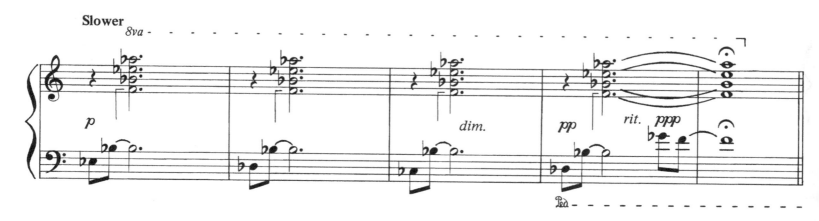

Sonata

PIANO REDUCTION AND EDITING
BY JACKSON BERKEY

COMPOSED BY CHIP DAVIS

Moderato, ♩ = c. 84

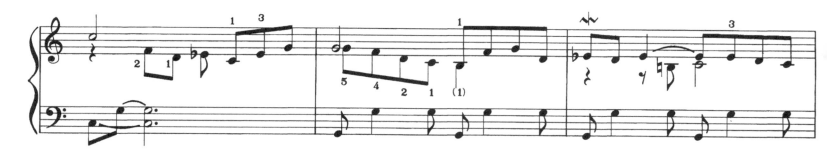

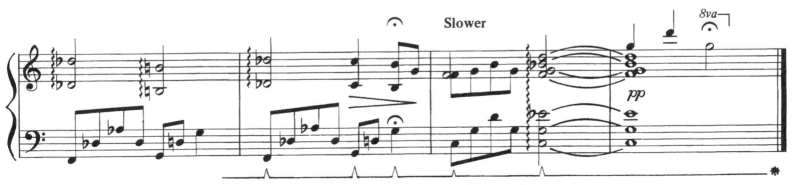

* Play the top right hand note with the beginning of the left hand rolled chord.
The rolled chord should be played as sixteenth notes.

Interlude 2

PIANO REDUCTION AND EDITING
BY JACKSON BERKEY

COMPOSED BY CHIP DAVIS

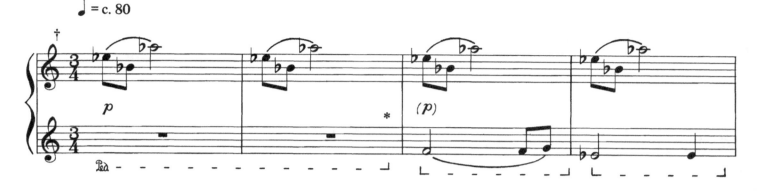

† Interlude 2 uses a three-note ostinato pattern in the right hand.

* On a grand piano, the strings inside the instrument may be plucked for the left hand notes through measure 9.
The left hand should return to the keyboard in measure 9.

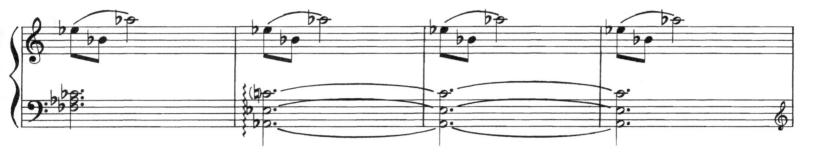

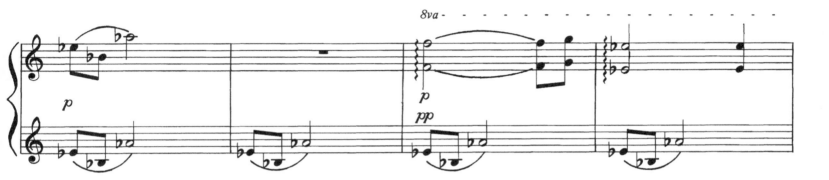

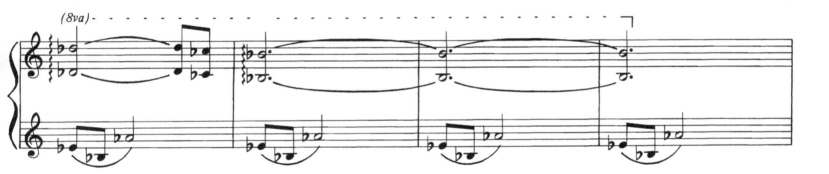

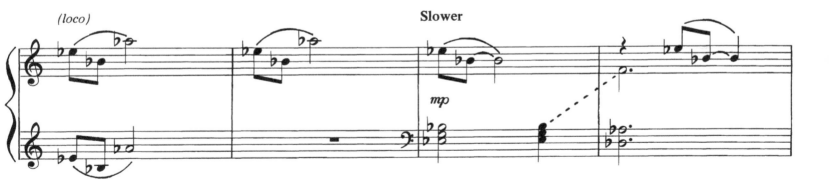

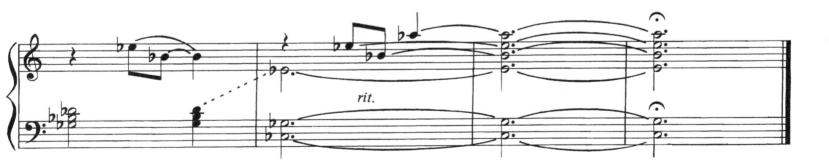

Sara's Band

PIANO REDUCTION AND EDITING
BY JACKSON BERKEY

COMPOSED BY CHIP DAVIS

Angular, Rock Style

* Pedal may be used sparingly to enhance the longer notes of the ostinato pattern, but it must not interfere with the melodic articulation.

Swing Feel

Even 8ths

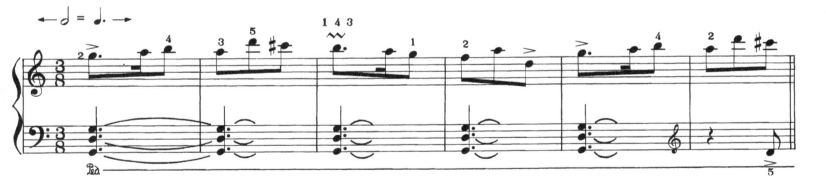

*Right hand may be played *8va* higher from here to the end, on the final repeat.

Fresh Aire

PIANO REDUCTION AND EDITING
BY JACKSON BERKEY

COMPOSED BY CHIP DAVIS

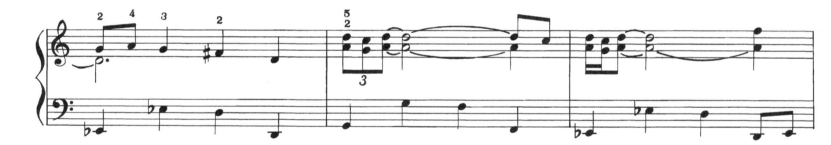

* Omit the 𝄢 B - flat if it cannot be reached.

* Omit the 𝄢 B - flat if it cannot be reached.

Ron Doe

PIANO REDUCTION AND EDITING
BY JACKSON BERKEY

COMPOSED BY CHIP DAVIS

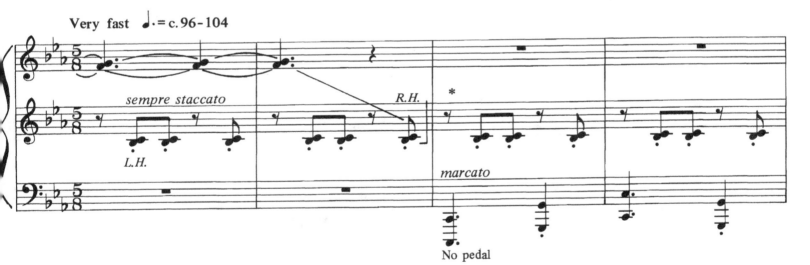

* Take middle stave notes in the right hand.

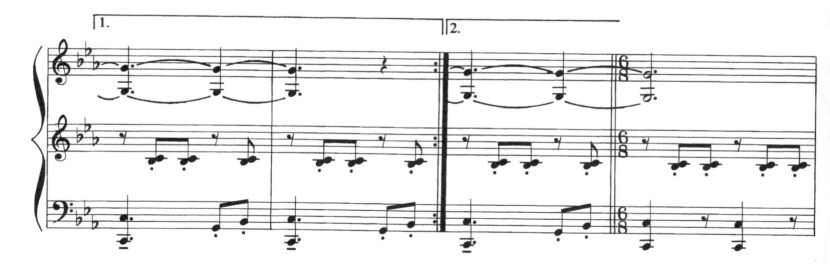

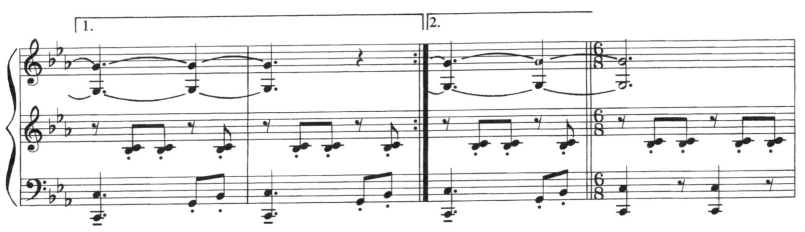

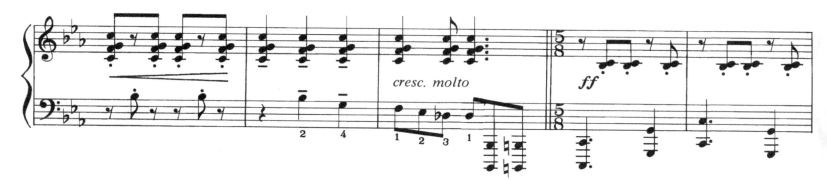

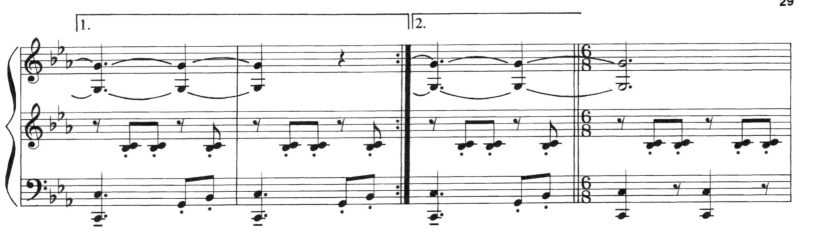

* Hold to end with sostenuto pedal.
** Left hand plays middle stave in this section.

Release sostenuto pedal with sustaining pedal.

Interlude 3

PIANO REDUCTION AND EDITING
BY JACKSON BERKEY

COMPOSED BY CHIP DAVIS

† Interlude 3 uses a two-note ostinato pattern in the left hand.

Pass the Keg, Lia

PIANO REDUCTION AND EDITING
BY JACKSON BERKEY

COMPOSED BY CHIP DAVIS

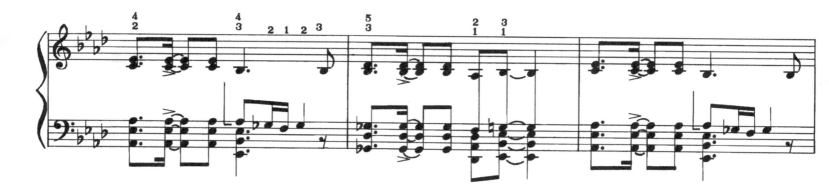

Interlude 4

PIANO REDUCTION AND EDITING
BY JACKSON BERKEY

COMPOSED BY CHIP DAVIS

Mist

PIANO REDUCTION AND EDITING
BY JACKSON BERKEY

COMPOSED BY CHIP DAVIS

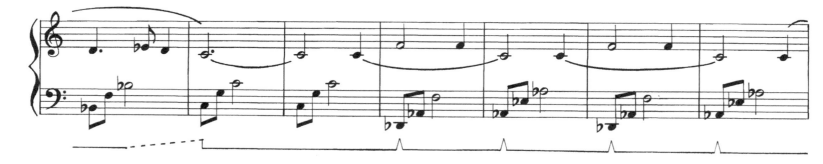

* The E♭ and D may be taken in the left hand.